Jim is 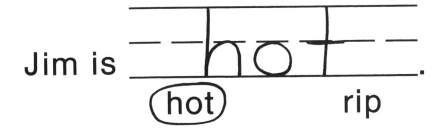 .

( hot )     rip

Al has a bag of _____ .

lap          nuts

The wig is in a _____ .

hit          box

Ann is not a _____ .

man          ran

1

Pam has a big pan. It is a pan of ham. The pan is too hot.

But Pam has a hot pad. She can pick up the pan with the hot pad.

---

Pam has a pan 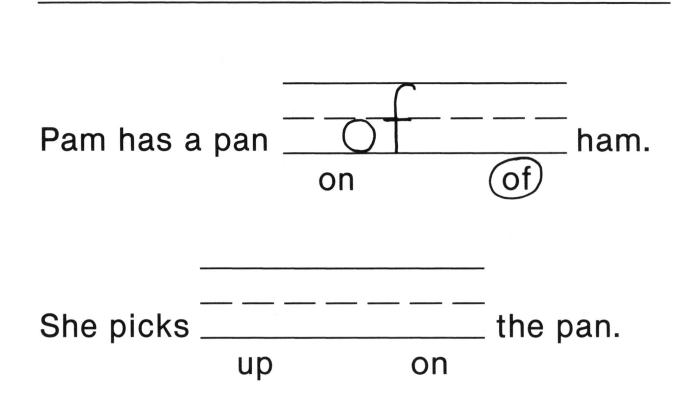 ham.
on    (of)

She picks _____ the pan.
up    on

It is tan. Jill can fill it up. It has a lid.

But it is not a pan, and it is not a pot.

Jill's cat can sit in it.

It is a 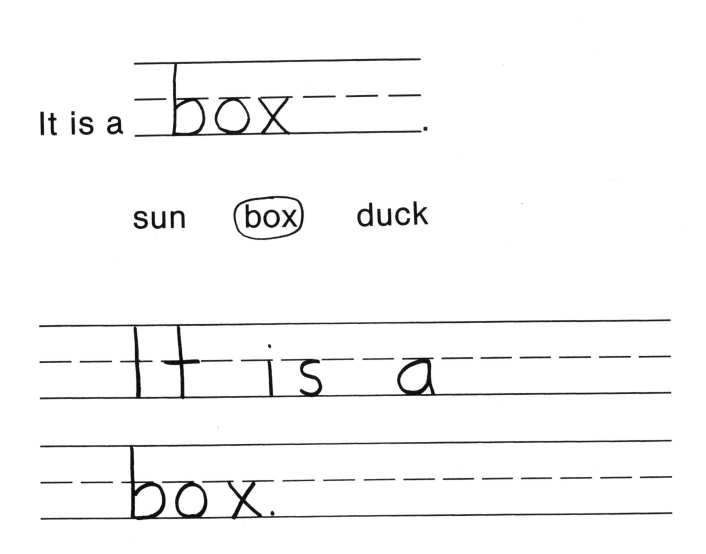box.

sun (box) duck

It is a box.

# 1, 2, or X ?

_1_ Jack runs to a box.

_X_ The bag is red.

_2_ Jack picks up the lid of the box.

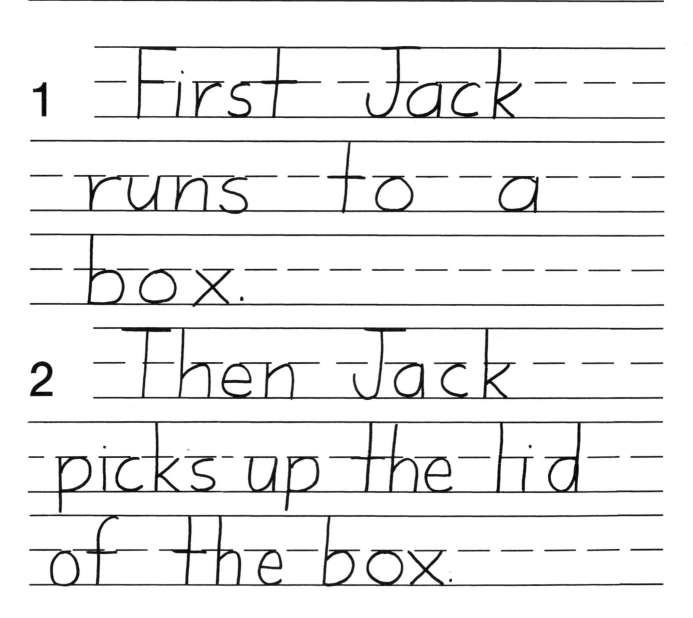

1 First Jack runs to a box.

2 Then Jack picks up the lid of the box.

Jill got a big _____.

hot        doll

Don can run and _____.

hop        gum

Ron can _____.

jog        doll

Dad naps on a _____.

luck        cot

Ron got a bag of nuts. He hid the bag of nuts in a box. The box fit in back of his cot.

But the pup ran in and got the nuts. Then Ron got the bag, but the pup had the nuts.

---

Ron hid the _____.

cot      bag

The pup got the _____.

man      nuts

It digs in the mud. It sits and naps in the hot sun. But it can not hop. It is too big and fat.

_____

It is a _____.

cot     bus     pig

_____

_____

_____

_____

# 1, 2, or X ?

___ The pup dug a pit.

___ Mom can't run in the fog.

___ Dad filled the pit back in.

1 first

2 Then

A pig is a _____.

            hop        hog

A doll can't _____.

            run        Ron

The sun got _____.

            fox        hot

The cat ran to the _____.

            fox        hot

Jill has a big doll. The doll has

a tan wig. The doll has lots of hats, too.

The doll can sit, but it can't run.

Jill hugs the doll and has fun with it.

_____

The doll has _____ of hats.

          lots     boxes

Jill has lots of _____.

          dolls     fun

It is tin. It can fit on a pan. It can fit on a pot, too.

Don can pick it up if it is not too hot. It is not a can.

It is a _____.

can    lid    pup

# 1, 2, or X ?

___ The bin is locked.

___ Don sat in the back of the bus.

___ Don got on the bus.

1 first

2 Then

The fox sat on a _____ .

of          rock

Nan naps on the _____ .

fog          cot

Ron has six _____ .

dolls          jogs

The sun is big and _____ .

got          hot

The fox digs a pit for its pups. The fox's pups nap in the pit. The fox licks the pups as they sit in the pit.

Then a cub jumps into the pit. The fox hops up and nips the cub. The cub yaps and runs to its mom.

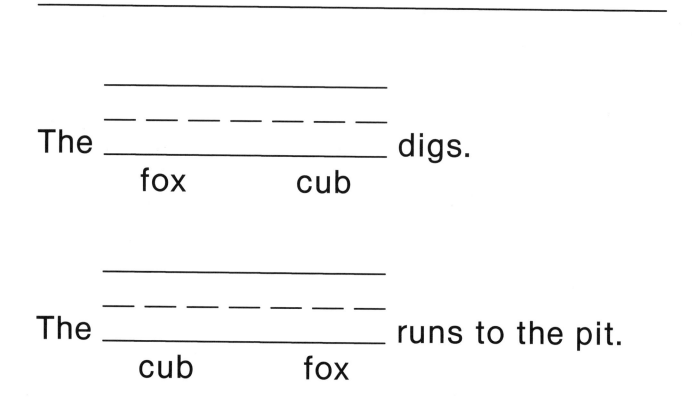

The _____ digs.
        fox        cub

The _____ runs to the pit.
        cub        fox

You can sit on it. You can put a cot on it. It has fuzz on it, too. Pups and cats can nap on it. It is not a pad.

_____

It is a _____.

rug      fox      nap

_____

_____

_____

# 1, 2, or X ?

___ Dad taps Mom on the back.

___ Ron got a big box.

___ Ron filled up the box.

1  first

2  Then

Ann and Bob can _____.

jog        hot

The ham is in the _____.

hop        pot

Pat hugs Dad and _____.

Mom        jog

The pups have _____.

fun        hog

The kids got cans of pop. They tip the pop into big mugs. Then the kids sip the mugs of pop.

The pop fizzes in the mugs. It is fun to sip it.

_____

It is fun to _____ the pop.

               tip        sip

The kids have mugs of _____.

                  cans      pop

It is tin. It can have a lid, but it is not a box.

You can put ham in it, but it is not a can. It is a big pan.

_____

It is a _____.

pot     bag     man

_____

_____

_____

# 1, 2, or X ?

___ Liz got the pot of ham hot.

___ It is fun to hop to jazz.

___ Liz had a pot of ham.

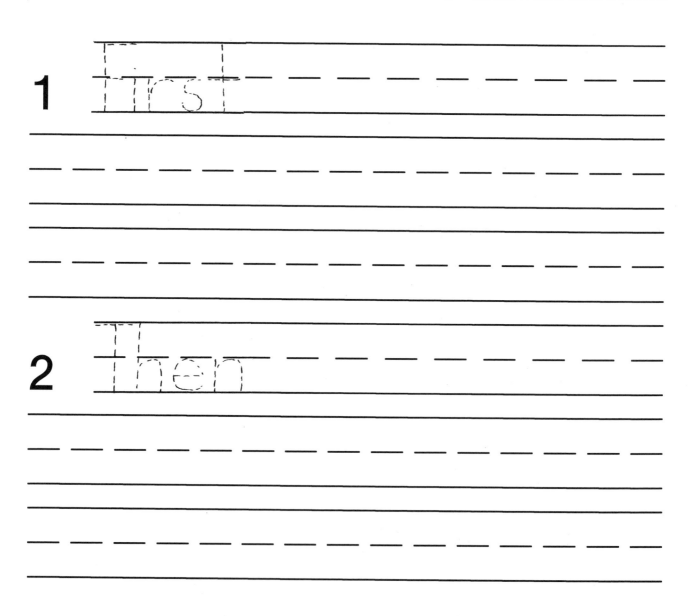

1   first

2   Then

The cat licks _____.

lock       Gus

Bill's pal is _____.

cot       Tom

Todd has on tan _____.

socks       hug

Mom and Dad have lots of _____.

pots       big

Tom is a big man. He has lots of big, tan socks. He puts the socks in a box. The big socks fit Tom.

Tom has big _____.
socks     pigs

The socks _____ Tom.
rub          fit

It can sit on a kid's bed, but it is not Mom or Dad. You can put a hat and socks on it. It can have a bib on, too.

But it can't hop or have a job.

_____

It is a _____.

Tom     doll     pot

_____

_____

_____

_____

# 1, 2, or X ?

___ The cat runs to Tom's sock.

___ The cat naps on Tom's sock.

___ The gull sits on the dock.

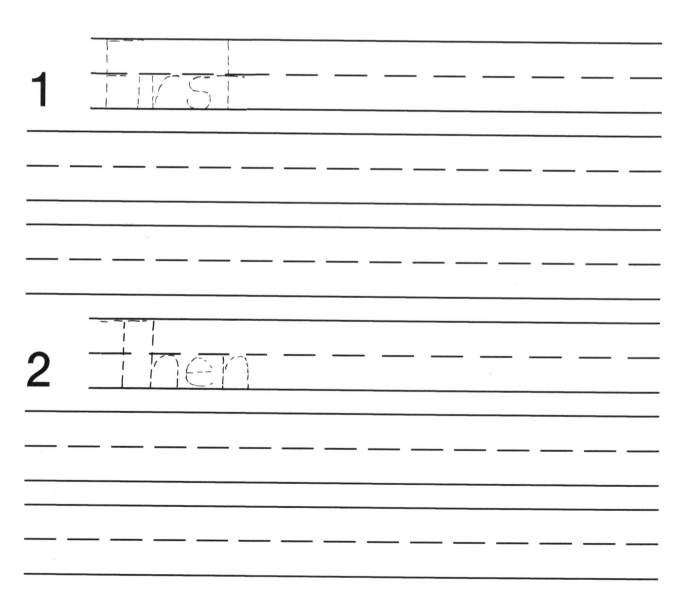

1 First

2 Then

The fox sits _____.

nod            up

Dot is Jim's _____.

mom            fog

The big ox _____.

dot            naps

The lid is on top of the _____.

luck            pot

A big bus has to putt-putt up the hill.

At first a hot rod is in back of the bus,

but then it passes it. At the top of the

hill the hot rod can not go. It has no gas.

Then the bus passes the hot rod.

---

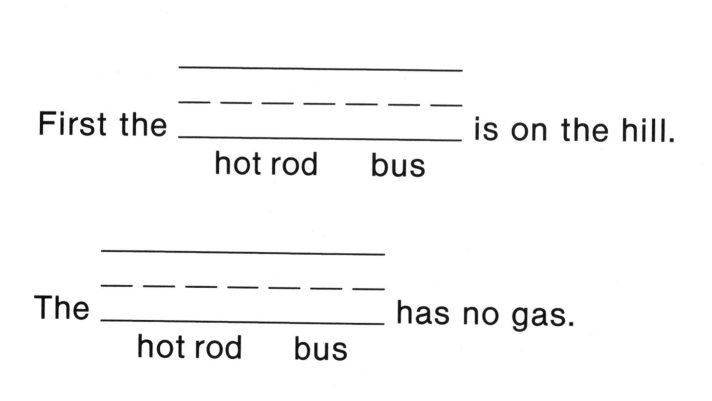

First the _____ is on the hill.

           hot rod    bus

The _____ has no gas.

    hot rod    bus

It fits on top of Don or Ann, but it is not a wig. A man can put it on, and tip it back. It can have a pin in it, but it is not a rip.

_____

It is a _____.

dot     lid     hat

_____

_____

_____

# 1, 2, or X ?

___ The kids hum to Dad and Mom.

___ The ox got mad at the bug.

___ A bug bit an ox on the back.

1   first

2   Then

The man is a _____.

         mop        cop

Mom puts the sock on _____.

         lick        Tom

Dot runs to the _____.

         fun        cab

The fox runs and _____.

         kicks        top

Mom sits on the dock in the sun. She has a sack of buns. A big gull hops on the dock. Mom tosses it a bit of bun. It picks it up.

Mom is on the _____.

rock    dock

The gull got the _____.

cod    bun

It has a top, but it is not a box or a pan. It is big.

A cat can run on it, and Bob can jog on it, too. But it is not a rug, and it is not a mat.

_____

It is a _____.

rug          hill          job

_____

_____

_____

# 1, 2, or X ?

___ Mom fixed the rips.

___ Dad dips a bun in the jam.

___ Mom's socks had big rips.

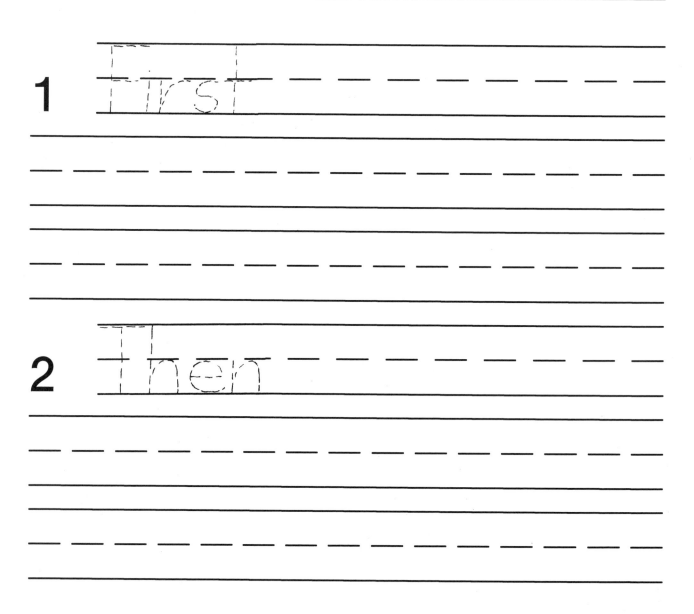

1   First

2   Then

The fox sat on a big _____.

rock        nip

Bob said, "I am _____."

Tom        Bob

Mom cut the _____.

log        fog

The man is in the _____.

fill        cab

Dad said, "I am mad. I am mad at the fox. The fox got the jam."

Dad ran and ran, but he did not nab the fox.

---

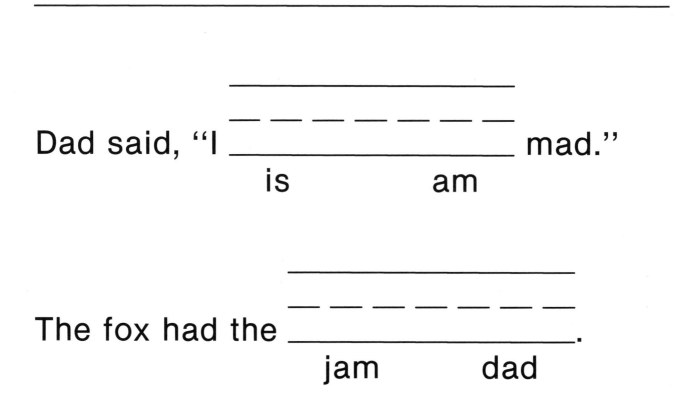

Dad said, "I _____ mad."
               is          am

The fox had the _____.
               jam        dad

It is big and tan. An ax can cut it up.
You can sit on it. It can have moss on it.

_____

It is a _____.

log      pup      dot

_____

_____

# 1, 2, or X ?

___ The pup ran to the man.

___ Sal has six jacks.

___ The pup licked the man.

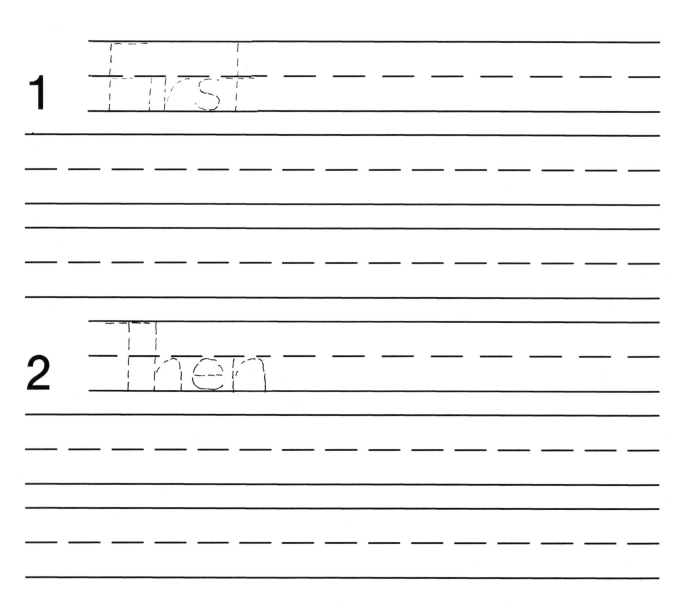

1 first

2 Then

The box has a _____.

top      hop

A big pig is a _____.

lock      hog

Tom did his _____.

job      sub

Jill and Tom had _____.

fun      did

Mom said, "Dot has a big job. She will cut up the log."

Dot said, "I can cut it up."

Dot got the ax and did the job. Then she sat in the sun.

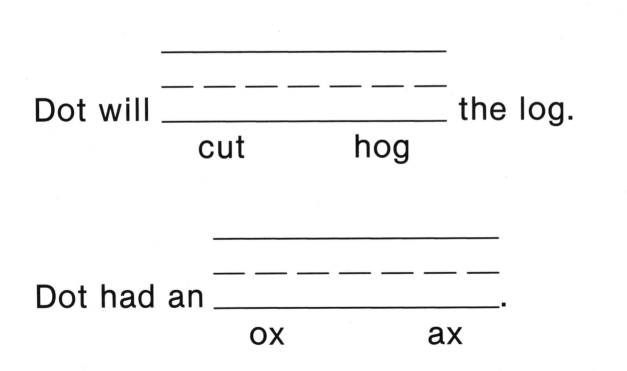

Dot will _____ the log.
          cut        hog

Dot had an _____.
         ox        ax

It is in a hot rod, but it is not Mom or Dad. A van has to have it or it will not run.

It is bad to sip it, and it will pop if it is lit.

_____

It is  _____.

a man     a van     gas

_____

# 1, 2, or X ?

___ The fox got the bun.

___ Don hid his bun in a hat.

___ Ann fans the man.

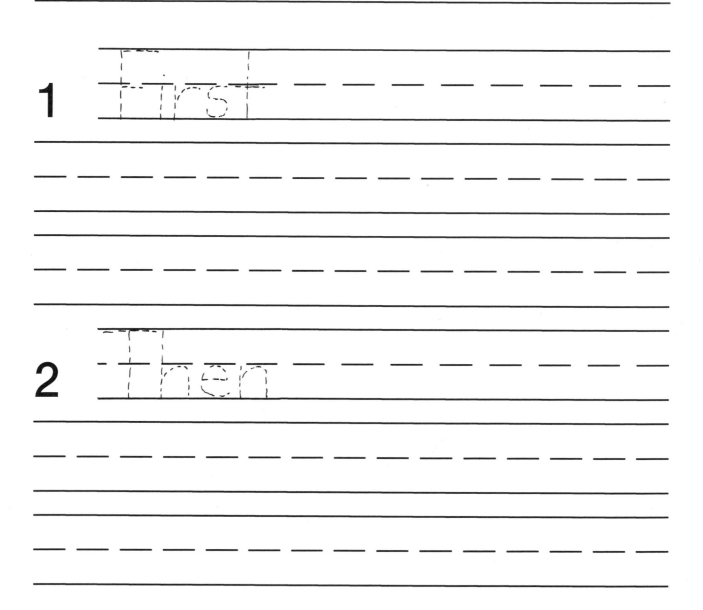

1  first

2  Then

Jill is a _____.

        mop      cop

Don mops up the _____.

        mud      lip

The ram sat on a big _____.

        rock      hit

Ann did a big _____.

        fog      job

Dad said, "A bit of jam is on the rug."

Bob said, "I will mop it up." But then the pup licked up the jam.

Bob said, "I will pat the pup. She did the job for me."

---

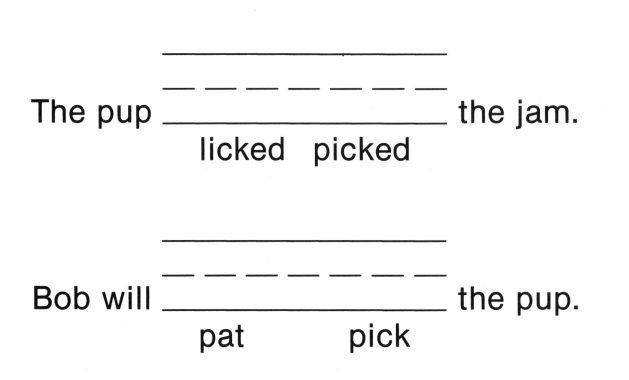

The pup _____ the jam.
　　　　　licked　picked

Bob will _____ the pup.
　　　　　pat　　　　pick

Dad and Mom can sit in it, but it is not big. It has gas in it, but it is not a bus, a van, or a cab.

It can pass cabs. It can zip up a hill.

_____

It is a _____.

cab    bin    hot rod

_____

_____

_____

_____

_____

# 1, 2, or X ?

___ The kid has a kit.

___ Mud got on Dot's rug.

___ Dot mops up the mud.

1  First

2  Then

The fan is on a _____.

hid     box

Bob and Don have lots of _____.

fun     dot

The ox tugs on the _____.

sad     log

Mom has a rag and a _____.

mop     rid

The man runs to the bus. But the bus passes him. The man misses the bus. He is mad.

Then the man has to run to his job.

_____

The man is _____.
                 sad       mad

The man _____ the bus.
          misses   passes

Bob can nap on it, and Mom can nap on it, too. It is not as big as a bed. It has a mat on top of it. It is on the rug.

_____

It is a _____.

sun        cot        lid

_____

_____

# 1, 2, or X ?

___ Then Tom said, "I have the rock."

___ Tom picked up the rock.

___ The pup tugs on Pam's cuff.

1 First

2 Then

The cat is Bob's _____.

pet        sock

Mom said, "Yes, I _____."

cot        will

Deb and Bob are _____.

pop        pals

The pots and pans are _____.

hop        tin

The bugs are buzzing on the pup's neck. The pup yaps. He rubs his neck on the rock. Tom yells to Meg, "I bet a bug bit the pup."

_____

The bug nips the _____.

                            pup        kids

The pup _____.

                bit        yaps

She can hug and kiss. She can hum and yell, too. She has a mom and a dad. She can get sick and get well. She has socks and hats.

_____

She is _____.
___ ___ ___ ___ ___ ___ ___

Deb     Bob     ox

_____
___ ___ ___ ___ ___ ___ ___ ___
_____
___ ___ ___ ___ ___ ___ ___ ___
_____

# 1, 2, or X ?

___ Dad fell on the dock.

___ Jan met Jeff.

___ Dad yelled to Mom.

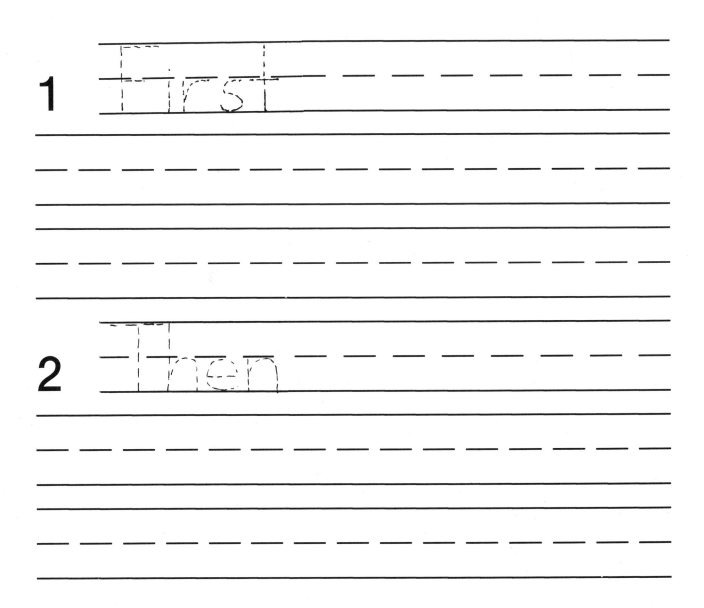

1   First

2   Then

Mud is _____.

wet      hot

Don's dad is _____.

jet      Ken

Don's mom is _____.

egg      Peg

Nan will get the _____.

cups      at

First the pups are licking Ken's doll.

Ken gets a rag and rubs the doll.

Then the pups get on Ken and lick him. Ken hugs the pups.

Ken and the pups have fun.

---

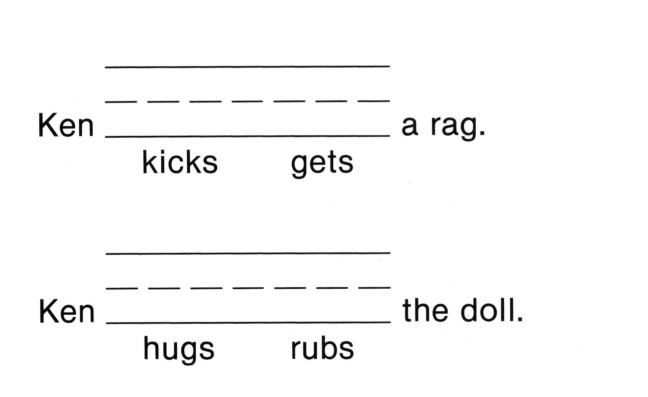

Ken _____ a rag.
     kicks     gets

Ken _____ the doll.
     hugs     rubs

It is red and tan. It can get hens, ducks, eggs, and nuts. It is not a cub.

It can get pups in its den, but it is not a dog.

_____

It is a _____.

fox     cub     hen

_____

_____

_____

# 1, 2, or X ?

___ Peg picked up the fan.

___ Kim ran on the dam.

___ Peg's fan fell in the mud.

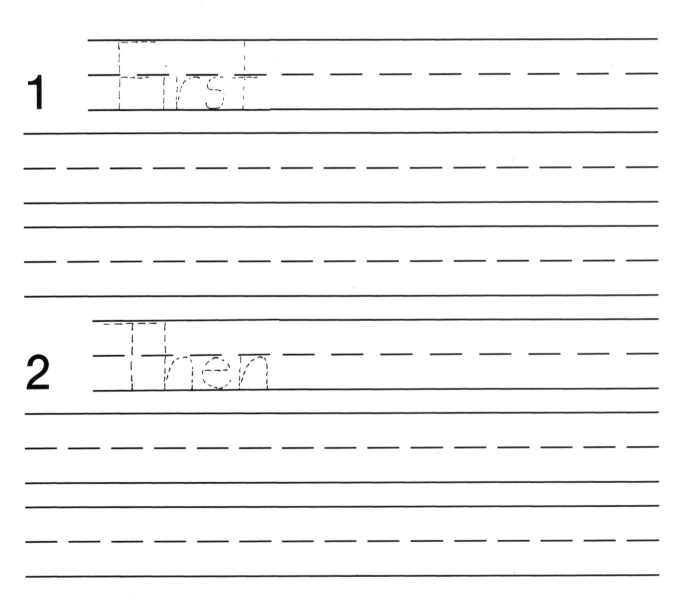

1 First

2 Then

The van is in the _____.

fog        rid

Tom naps on the _____.

bed        him

Dick and Pam have a T.V. _____.

six        set

The bug bit Ken's _____.

neck        us

Matt has a bit of red gum. He has the gum on his lips. "The gum will not pop," he said.

But the gum gets too big, and it pops! Then Matt has lots of gum on him.

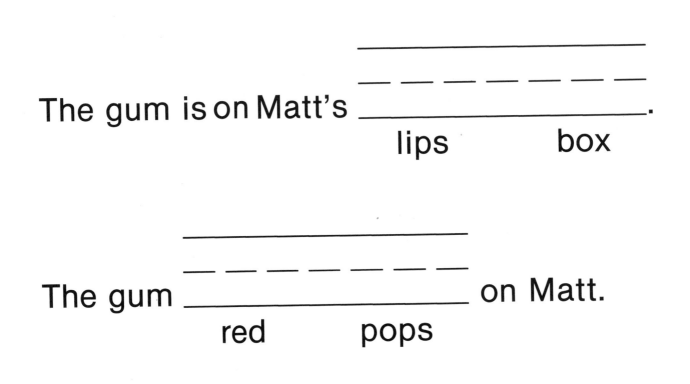

The gum is on Matt's _____.
lips        box

The gum _____ on Matt.
red        pops

He hugs Mom and the kids. He can sip pop, and he can add. He can mop, and he can fix the T.V. set.

If he gets sick, he can't get well at the vet's. He is a man.

He is _____.

Jeff   the vet   Dad

# 1, 2, or X ?

___ Russ sits on the deck.

___ Jeff wins the bet.

___ Bob and Jeff have a bet.

1  first

2  Then

Dad mops up the _____.

cop      mess

Ken got a set of tin _____.

men      red

Peg's hog has a fat _____.

neck      lid

Deb said, " _____, I will."

Yes      As

Peg, Sid, and Jack are in the lot. Peg runs up to Jack and tags him. "You are 'It,' " she yells, and runs. Then Jack runs to get Sid. But he misses.

Peg tags _____ .

        Sid       Jack

The kids are in the _____ .

        van       lot

It has legs, but it is not a dog or a cat. It has a top, but not a lid. You can get up on it and have a nap.

_____

It is a _____.

bed    rock    neck

_____

_____

_____

# 1, 2, or X ?

___ The bell fell into the tub.

___ The bell got wet.

___ The kid has lots of pets.

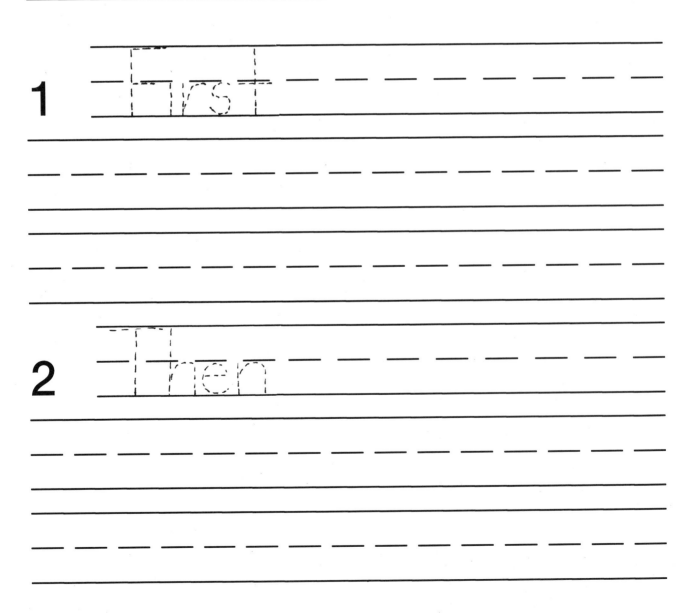

1 First

2 Then

The van was _____.

egg          red

Mom said, "I will kiss _____."

at          you

A pup is a _____.

pet          bed

Dad tells Deb to _____.

set          nap

Peg had a big box. The box was up to Ken's neck. Ken said to Peg, "You have a big box."

"Yes," said Peg. "It has a T.V. set in it."

Ken said, "Is the T.V. set as big as I am, too?"

_____

The box was as big as _____.
pets          Ken

Peg has a _____.
T.V. set          hen

It is a pet. It runs and hops, and it sits and wags, too. It licks you and you can hug it. But it is not a cat.

_____

It is a _____.

fox     pup     mop

# 1, 2, or X ?

___ Sid said, "Will you fix the T.V.?"

___ Dad sells his van.

___ Mom fixed the T.V. set.

1 First

2 Then

The cop's pen is _____.

Bob       red

The big bell was _____.

tin       fell

Jack has ten _____.

jog       maps

Jill has red _____.

dig       lips

The man's duck has tan legs, but its back and neck are red.

The duck sits in lots of mud.

The mud gets on its back and neck.

Then its back and neck are tan, too.

---

The duck's legs are _____.
red      tan

The mud gets on the _____.
man      duck

It is red. It is wet, but you can't sip it. You can put it on a bun, and you can lick it.

It is not ham.

_____

It is _____.

bell     cup     jam

_____

_____

# 1, 2, or X ?

___ The rug has fuzz on it.

___ The cop got the men.

___ The cop ran to the men.

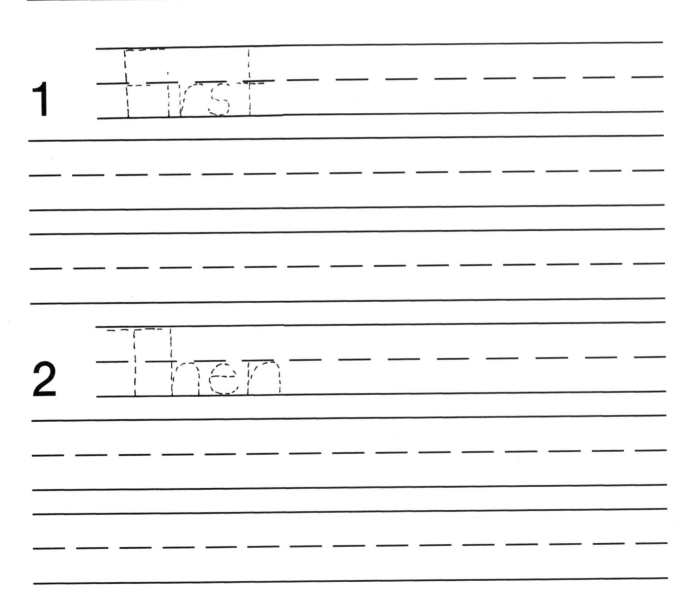

1  first

2  Then

Jeff gets a T.V. _____.

           set        net

The pet in the tub got _____.

           wet        fat

Ron has six _____.

           let        pens

The bug has ten _____.

           socks        legs

First Jeff tells his dog Sam to run.
Sam gets up to run.

But then the dog hits its leg on a
rock and gets a big cut.

Jeff tells Sam to sit. Then he
fixes the cut.

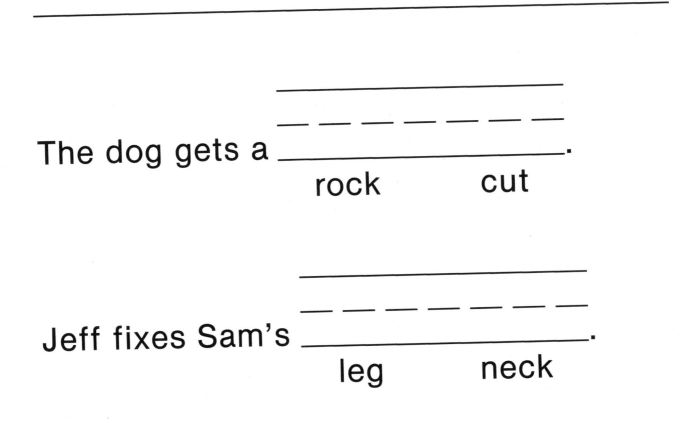

The dog gets a _____.
rock          cut

Jeff fixes Sam's _____.
leg          neck

You can fill it up, but it is not a cup or a box. You can sit in it, but it is not a van.

You get wet in it, and you can have fun in it, but it is not mud.

It is a _____.

bell    mat    tub

# 1, 2, or X ?

___ She gets wet.

___ Mom tucks Lil into bed.

___ Bev gets into the tub.

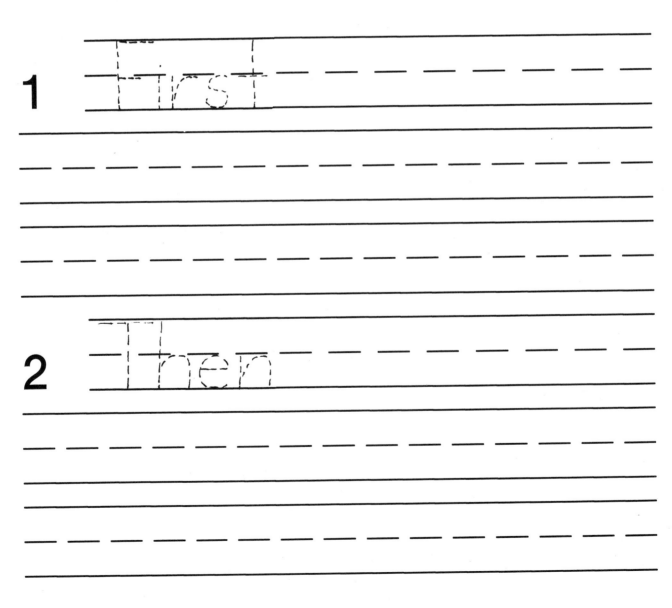

1 First

2 Then

Ken hops on his _____.

leg       can't

The pup _____.

wigs      digs

Ten cabs pass the _____.

run      bus

The bell is _____.

red      van

Don's cat was big and tan. It had a red bell on its neck. The cat got up on Don's bed.

The bell hit Don's cup, and the cup fell on the rug. But Don was not mad.

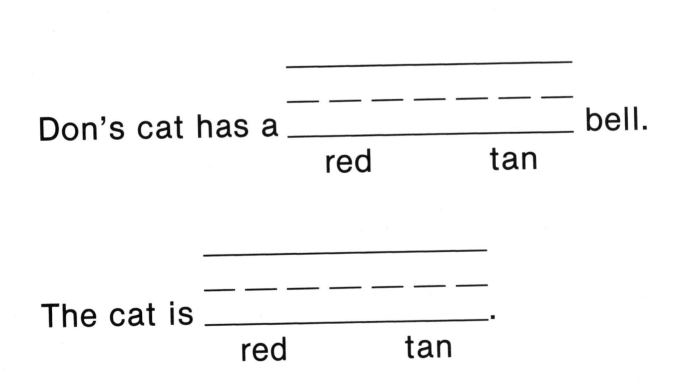

Don's cat has a _____ bell.

red       tan

The cat is _____.

red       tan

It can go up but it is not a gull. It is big. Mom and Dad can sit in it, but it is not a bus. Kids can sit in it, too. It has to have gas to go up. It has gas in it.

_____

It is a _____.

ball      jet      bus

_____

_____

_____

# 1, 2, or X ?

___ Dick puts six buns in a pan.

___ The bus is in a rut.

___ The buns get hot in the pan.

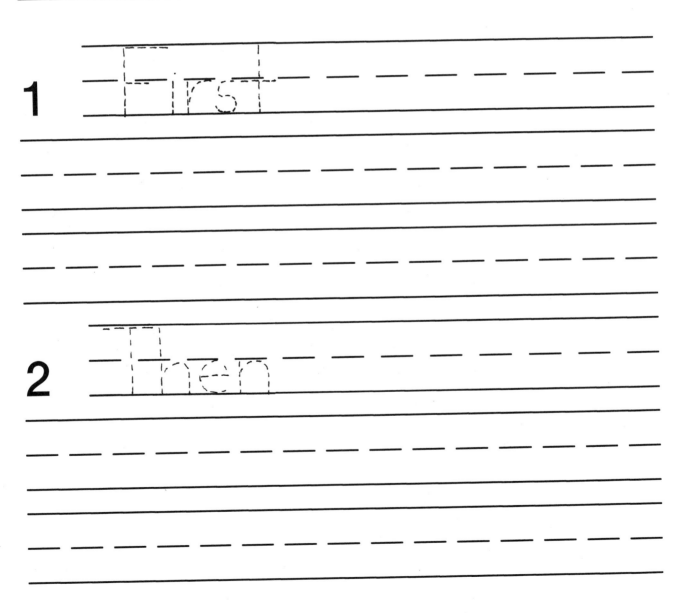

1 First

2 Then

Jill has a big _____.

         hen       red

Hens sit on _____.

         eggs       buses

They are _____.

         men       hit

The man has a _____.

         yes       mop

Deb and Peg are pals. They have lots of fun.

First they have fun with jacks.

Then they put hats on Deb's doll.

Deb tells Peg, "I have fun with you."

---

Deb and Peg are _____.

                pals        fat

They pick up _____.

           tubs      jacks

They are red and tan. They sit on eggs. They can dig in the mud and they can peck at you. They are not ducks.

_____

They are _____.

rags     hens     ducks

_____

_____

_____

_____

# 1, 2, or X ?

___ The bass has fins.

___ Ron mops up the mess.

___ The eggs fell on the rug.

1  First

2  Then

Dad said, "Let's go to _____."

bed        hen

Dick hit the rock and _____.

ten        fell

Bill mops up the _____.

pet        mess

Dot can't get up _____.

yet        led

Ann gets a red pot for the ham. The pot has a big mess in it. Ann gets rid of the mess with a wet rag. Then she sets the ham in the pot.

_____

The pot is _____.
       wet       red

Ann gets a _____.
       rag       mop

It was tan and wet. Nan and Tom
fell into it. It was a big, wet mess. It got
on Nan and Tom. They had to get in the
tub to get rid of it.

_____

It was _____.

mud     rug     hens

_____

_____

# 1, 2, or X ?

___ They passed the bus.

___ Mom and Dad got into the van.

___ Meg picks a fig.

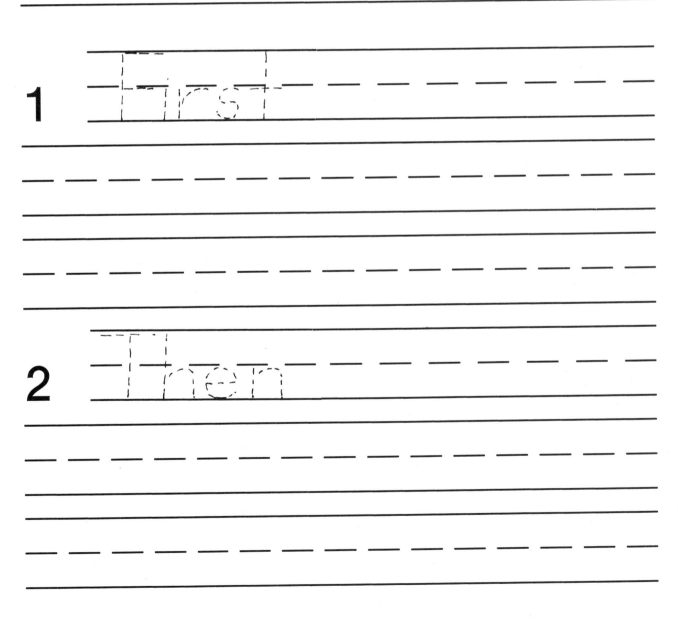

1 first

2 Then

The bus has a _____.

       neck      bell

Peg did the job _____.

       well      jet

Ten men _____ into the pit.

       fell      yet

The sick men got _____.

       tell      well

The men have a big job. They have to fix the cop's van.

First Ed gets a can of gas, but the van will not run yet. Then Ben tugs on the van with a rod, and he fixes it.

Ben tugs with the _____.

                      bat        rod

Ed gets _____.

             vans       gas

You can have it in a cup or a mug. You can sip it, but it is not pop.

It has lots of eggs in it, but it is not a hen's hut. It is not a bun, and it is not ham and eggs.

_____

It is _____.

egg nog    bun    hen

_____

_____

_____

# 1, 2, or X ?

___ Jeff filled the box with pens.

___ Sis can't sit up yet.

___ Jeff locked the box of pens.

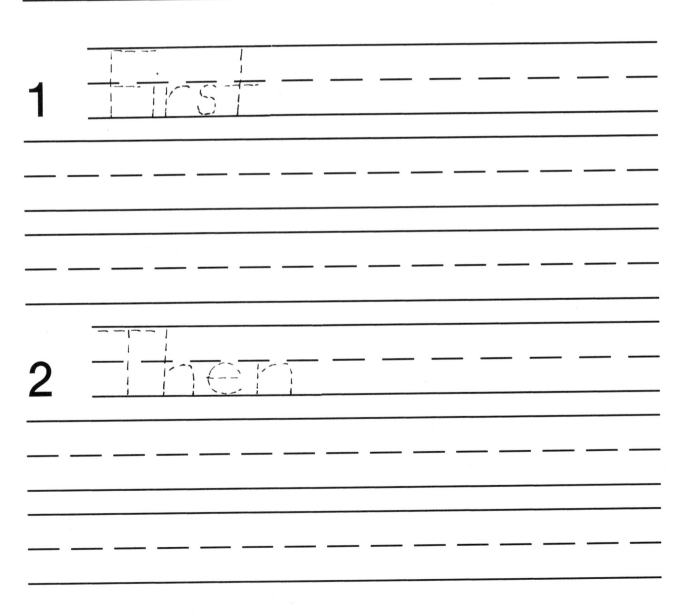

1  First

2  Then

Mom was in a _____.

       jet       get

The T.V. set is in the _____.

       ten       den

Peg fed the _____.

       well       pet

Dad gets in the _____.

       cab       nab

The pets get into Deb's backpack. First the pup tugs on Deb's map and rips it. Then the cat digs in the pack and gets Deb's pad and red pen. It is a big mess!

_____

The pup rips the _____.

socks    map

The cat gets the _____.

pen    pup

They are in sets. They fit on legs. They fit on Jill and Bill, but they can't fit on hens.

_____

They are _____.

maps        hats        socks

_____

_____

_____

# 1, 2, or X ?

___ Peg fed the pet.

___ Peg got a pet.

___ The bugs buzz on the hut.

1  First

2  Then